How to Analyze People

Read People Instantly Using Psychological Techniques, Social Skills, and Body Language Signals

By Lucas Garrison

The content and information contained in this book have been compiled from sources deemed reliable, and it is accurate to the best of the Author's knowledge, information, and belief. However, the Author cannot guarantee its accuracy and validity and cannot be held liable for any errors and/or omissions. Further, changes are periodically made to this book as and when needed. Where appropriate and/or necessary, you must consult a professional (including but not limited to your doctor, attorney, financial advisor or such other professional advisor) before using any of the suggested remedies, techniques, or information in this book.

Upon using the contents and information contained in this book, you agree to hold harmless the Author from and against any damages, costs, and expenses, including any legal fees potentially resulting from the application of any of the information provided by this book.

This disclaimer applies to any loss, damages or injury caused by the use and application, whether directly or indirectly, of any advice or information presented, whether for breach of contract, tort, negligence, personal injury, criminal intent, or under any other cause of action.

You agree to accept all risks of using the information presented inside this book.

You agree that by continuing to read this book, where appropriate and/or necessary, you shall consult a professional (including but not limited to your doctor, attorney, or financial advisor or such other advisor as needed) before using any of the suggested remedies, techniques, or information in this book.

Table Of Contents

Introduction

What if you could read people's minds? Imagine how different your life could be if you could effortlessly read people: if you could quickly tell what people were thinking, what they wanted, and how to interact with them. From business to family functions, to daily interactions on the street, we are constantly moving through and around different kinds of people. What are they thinking? What are they feeling? How will they receive us? How can we maximize our ability to understand people in order to be more compassionate members of our various communities, as well as able to meet our own financial and emotional needs?

This manual is an introduction to how to read people thoroughly and quickly. Of course, we aren't actually able to read minds, and everybody's inner workings are ultimately known only to themselves, but we are all constantly leaving clues for other people. We are all constantly showing our inner thoughts and needs by the actions of-of our bodies, our voices, and what we say. This is a guide to learning to track those clues and apply them to practical, real-life scenarios.

Before we begin...

Tips and Tricks for Making
Meaningful Connections and
Interpreting People's Behavior

You are not neutral

Before we start talking about how to read other people, let's turn the camera on ourselves for a moment. We often imagine that we see or hear is observed without bias. It is, after all, just what's happening. It's objective. But it's critical to understand that this is actually never true; all our own nuanced cultural, social, and educational backgrounds are constantly at play, even in the most simple moments. These factors tell us what to look at, dictates what we see when we look and brings us to conclusions about what we are experiencing before we even have time to consciously intervene, or see it as "bias". Of course, how this plays out will be radically different for everyone, because no two people have an identical background, and even people who are from similar background might choose to interact very differently with parallel experiences. Because of this, it's critical that we each do our own self-examination before thinking about other people and their behavior, and begin to understand our own unique perspective on the world.

Here are some questions that might prove useful

- **What are your contributing identity markers?** Age, gender identification, socio-demographic background, racial identity, etc? How do these factors shape

how do you see the world? What groups do you naturally feel at ease with, and which do you not?

This is obviously a very complex set of questions, that would require a lot of deep thought and a lot of reflection. Going down the path of deep self-exploration will only deepen your ability to practice these skills, but for the purposes of this manual, a brief exploration of the following questions will do.

- **What are the situations that you are primarily interested in learning to "read" people?** What are your motivating factors? It's easiest to read people if you are genuinely interested. You will approach somebody very differently if you are looking for them to invest money in your startup company than you would if you were trying to ask somebody on a date. Being honest about your intentions are very important, and will change how you approach somebody and the tactics that will be helpful to you. We'll get into the specific tactics later, but what's important at this stage is to be able to understand the difference in how YOU approach people when you have different intentions.

It has been proven that we hear and see in the people around us is more often than not based on what we expect to see, which is based on what we have seen before. In this way, it becomes obvious that we are constantly reproducing the world we already know. This can be very limiting to what we can see and understand about other people. This is why it's so important to spend some time thinking about the objective bias you bring to people, and it is also a great reason to quickly check in with yourself about what you are expecting to see and hear in specific situations where you are trying to read people. What you are expecting to see will infinitely inform what you do see.

Here's a sample profile that will illustrate this: let's say you grew up in rural Wyoming in a wealthy but isolated rich Protestant farming community and hadn't spent much time around the diversity of any kind. Your family valued hard work, modesty, and didn't make space for people talking about intense feelings. People from other religions and countries were completely absent from your world. Everybody you knew was a white Christian, pretty much exactly like you. You were almost never in a situation where you could get to know (and empathize) with people from different backgrounds. When you graduated from high school, you went to a state university, where you remained largely segregated. After you graduate, you got your dream job, working in financial investment. You were traveling for the first time, meeting lots of different kinds of people, and it was expected that you could connect with and easily read all these people. You might find yourself struggling to have an open mind about their lives, religion, etc. All you can see is how different they are than you. This is undoubtedly going to get in the way. An uninterrogated past and bias can be a real stumbling block for connecting with people.

It is in your best interest to honestly understand these things about yourself. All of our backgrounds deeply affect how we are able to meet the world, and if we don't see them clearly, we operate out of a biased deficit. It is incredibly valuable to us to understand our own bias and work against them by practicing approaching different kinds of people with an open mind. This takes practice and strong self-awareness.

Reading Other People: Empathy

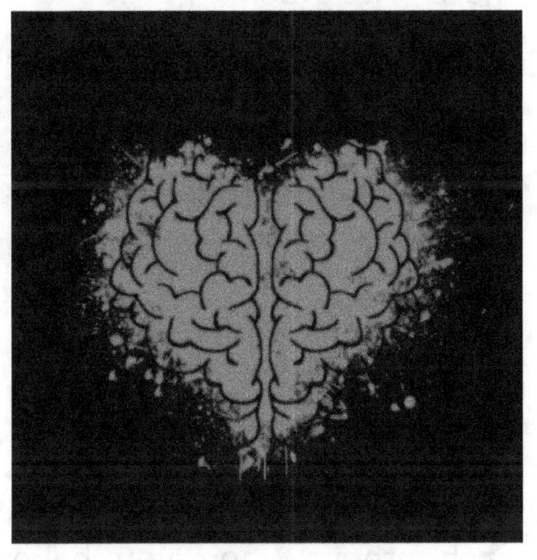

The core of reading other people lays in our innate ability to connect with other humans through empathetic and kinesthetic awareness. An empathetic connection between people is scientifically proven. When we are in conversation with somebody who we connect with, our breathing and heart rate sync up with the other person. The more we ask questions we genuinely care about and listen carefully to the answers, the more connected people feel, and the more aligned they become. This is how you quickly make friends and allies: by purposefully utilizing specific elements of our innate ability to connect with each other. When you have an empathetic connection with somebody, they instantly and deeply are drawn to you. This is commonly referred to as "charisma". This article is concerned with how that empathetic connection happens, and how we can recreate it purposefully.

The tricks and tips of this article are all based on the common principle of genuine empathy. At the core of this is an honest interest in other people. This is a skill that can be practiced and cultivated, but definitely, cannot be faked. As you read the following pages, remember that we already have the most valuable tool of all: the ability to empathize. You can begin to practice this instantly by observing people whenever you have a spare moment (parks and public transit are great for this) and allowing yourself to really see them. How are they sitting?

What do you think their lives are like? Allow yourself to practice this without judgment; just truly seeing what's there.

First Things First: Establish a Baseline

You will be most effective at reading people that you already know well because you understand their "baseline", or the nuanced ways that they act normally. A naturally extremely fidgety person may read to somebody who just met them as disingenuous or extremely uncomfortable, while a person who knows them well will understand that this is just their baseline, and would be able to read nuances in their behavior from that advantageous standpoint. There really is no replacement for a deep and genuine relationship with somebody, but when you don't have that, there are many strategies for still reading somebody well, which we will discuss below.

Make your Implicit Knowledge Explicit

When you are in situations where you have the advantage of knowing them well, use it! Study the people close to you and become familiar with their baseline. Articulate to yourself exactly what you observe about that person. I guarantee you already "know" these things implicitly, but you might find it oddly hard to state the specific baseline attributes of somebody that you know well. If I asked you right now to name what the person closest to you does when they are feeling nervous, you might feel like you don't know, but I guarantee you would recognize it when you see it. When you ask yourself to slow down and state what happens specifically and clearly, your implicit knowledge is becoming explicit or moving from subconscious to conscious. That way, if they start acting different, you will see it quickly and accurately. This is great practice for reading people quickly and accurately that you don't know well.

Obviously, many of the times you will be trying to read people is when you don't have the advantage of knowing them well, but there are still ways you can read people in these situations. You will be surprised how fast you'll be able to start to pick up on what is somebody's natural energy and when they are acting unusually. Humans are incredibly receptive creatures, and you'll find that you'll be able to start spotting a naturally nervous person versus a person in an unusual state of high nervousness with surprising accuracy. Your gut feelings should never be discounted. When you start paying attention, you'll see that you can pick up on somebody's natural energy within a few seconds of meeting them.

Depending on the situation, you also might be able to lean in on other people's strong relationships, and their knowledge of the person's baseline. Let's say that you are chatting with a small group of people from different companies at a networking event. One of the people is acting very nervous. While you have no way of knowing right away if this is somebody's baseline or unusual behavior, there are two things you should instantly do

1. Lean in on your gut feeling about if this is a nervous person or a person in a state of nervousness.

2. Try to discern if there is somebody else in this group who knows the person. A coworker, a partner, a friend- anybody more familiar with them than you are. How is that person interacting with the first person? If they are acting uncomfortable or unusually focused on the person, it is likely that

this is not baseline activity.

Even if you just met somebody, you can almost always find clues to the person's baseline by the way they are responding to their environment, and (just as importantly) how that person's environment is responding to them. The further from their baseline somebody is acting, the more intense their emotional response to what is being done or said.

How to Read What People Say

Much like with body language (which we'll get to later), what people say is not always just about what they are saying, but how they are saying it. It almost never matters what somebody says verbatim, but rather, the nuance of meaning is entirely in how they say it. Volume, speed, tone, pitch, and rhythm are all key to understanding what somebody is thinking.

The human ear is shockingly perceptive. It's almost impossible in words to describe the nuance in what we hear and how we interpret it. This is an innate skill we should constantly be using to our advantage. Again, this is much easier if you have a strong sense of the baseline of the person, but regardless, here are some general guidelines. As always, first and foremost, trust your gut, and start to practice making your intuitive knowledge explicitly known to you. You can start practicing this immediately. In your everyday life, start noticing how you feel about people as they communicate with you, and see if you can pinpoint what about their voice is making you feel that way. You'll notice that sometimes you have unusually strong feelings in fairly neutral situations. These are great moments to tune into and try to decipher.

For example, you go to a coffee shop, and after interacting with the barista, you think to yourself "I really like that person". The context is not meaningful or particularly memorable (getting coffee) but something about your interaction made you feel good. See if you can pinpoint what it is. Is it their eye contact? Did their tone sound warm? After reading this section you might have more language for what it is in these situations that make you feel good. It's equally valuable to pay attention to interactions that feel negative and try to identify how and how that happens.

Here are some specific elements of speech that are worth looking at specifically

Volume

First and foremost, volume can only be analyzed in context. Are you in a loud space where it's difficult to hear? Or a library? You would be shocked how often people overlook these huge environmental context factors, and you should always be aware of them. People never exist in a vacuum, and you'll find yourself at a great advantage if you read people's language in context.

In general, a greater volume means somebody has or is seeking power, and that they want to be heard. A quiet voice means they do not want to take up space, or that they are not comfortable with where they are in the power dynamics. A soft voice can be very powerful.

Tone and pitch

To read tone, you can almost exclusively rely on your intuitive ear. Notice how somebody's tone changes over the conversation. Notice the variance from their baseline. If you notice their tone harden, they are uncomfortable, while a softening tone is a great sign of greater intimacy and an opening up toward you.

The pitch goes up when somebody is insecure, looking for approval, angry, defensive, or feels powerless. In general, when the pitch goes up, it's because somebody is feeling powerless. They are either looking for power or looking for somebody else to take power and make them feel safe.

The pitch goes down when somebody feels confident, when they are romantically interested, when they are relaxed, or when they are angry. This is a power position. It means that they hold power, or they are very comfortable with how somebody else is holding power.

These things are always read in combination: a voice with low pitch and hard tone is very different than a low pitch and soft tone. You will find that you are already intuitively responding to these things, and when your attention is drawn to them, you can read nuance with great accuracy.

Speed

Somebody who is speaking fast is somebody who wants to be heard and has a concern that they won't be. This could be for a variety of reasons; their own insecurity to lack of power in the group, uncertainty about what they expressing, or a time-based situation (you're on an elevator and you are one floor away from their stop).

A slower speed often means that somebody is being more careful about what they are saying. Again, the reasons for this could be multifold and must be read in combination with each other, your gut feeling, what you understand of their baseline, and what's happening in the environment.

Word Choice

While the way that somebody speaks is critical, we also can't ever discount what somebody actually is saying. The specific language used gives you tons of clues about what people mean. To see how this works, let's look at an example. Let's say you are at an award ceremony for an organization you work for. You are chatting with a new colleague who is the recipient of a special medal for their work. You are just getting to know the person, and would really like to impress them and make a personal connection, but you have really only met a couple of times. In this conversation, what they say and how they say it will become major clues.

Let's examine a specific piece of information and how they choose to convey it for word clues: You congratulate them on their achievement. What they say next is critical. "I won an award" is the basic information they are conveying but, there are a variety of ways they might say this, and their word choice holds valuable clues about what they are thinking. Here are some examples and what they might mean.

- **"I really owe it to the hard work of my team".** Notice that they are referencing other people and teamwork rather than emphasizing themselves. Use this as an opportunity to ask them about the team, and affirm their ability to be a team player and leader.

- **"Awards don't matter, anyway"**. This person is looking for an opportunity to change the subject, or at least look like they are. They are uncomfortable with the focus being directly on their achievement. A great way to manage this potentially confusing moment is to instantly change the subject to something less focused on them, and then find a way to still affirm them, either in the new topic at hand, or by returning to the award at the end of the conversation with a quick, no string attached affirmation about their accomplishment.

- **"It was tricky to find the time to get the project done, but I did it".** It seems that this person is looking for an opportunity to talk about the other factors in their life that affected their time. Ask them what else they had going on, then take the opportunity to affirm that they sound really busy, and are obviously managing it really well.

From this example of a very simple phrase, you can see how information is always conveyed specifically, and that it matters deeply. If you listen closely, people tell you exactly how they want to be spoken to, it's just a matter of listening carefully and responding authentically.

Body Talk: How to Interpret Body Language

Body language is one of the most powerful tools of communication, and it makes itself instantly apparent. The moment you walk into a room, you are instantly taking in huge amounts of information about people. How somebody stands, their choices about eye contact, how they walk, what they do with their hands, all of these things are huge clues to what they are thinking, what they want, and how they move through the world.

Body language is a very powerful tool. We had body language before we had speech, and apparently, 80% of what you understand in a conversation is read through the body, not the words.

- Deborah Bull

New research tells us that up to 93% of the information we get from other people is non-verbal. This information is passing through our brains so quickly that we often don't even notice it happening, we just walk into a room and instantly feel the conclusions of this mass of information. This is often what's happening when you feel like you don't like or trust somebody, but you can't put your finger on why exactly.

It's incredibly beneficial to learn to slow down and tune in.

Here are some quick general tips on reading body language:

Positive signs

Signaling comfort, a desire to connect.

- Leaning toward you.
- Smiling with crinkled eyes.
- Turning toward somebody in conversation.
- Crossing legs toward you.
- Seeking out eye contact.

Negative signs

Signally discomfort, dishonesty, or a desire to leave.

- Crossed arms or legs.
- Smiles that do not crinkle the eyes.
- Continuously raising eyebrows.

- An unstable base; all the weight on one leg, or constantly shifting back and forth, while confidence comes with a strong base.

Here's the key to interpreting body language, however; you don't always know what exactly their body is responding to. None of us live in a bubble! For example, crossed arms signaling resistance might be in response to something that happened right before you walked in the room, or some internal factor that has nothing to do with you, or with a discomfort with their own body, or the temperature of the room. That is why body language is most successful when used in tandem with listening to what people are saying, and how they are saying it. Everything lives in a context, and it's crucial that you can tell not just how somebody is responding, but what they are responding to. Sometimes, you will notice that people are responding to the content of the conversation, and this is also important to pay attention to. For example, you might be getting all kinds of cues that somebody is excited to connect with you, and then as you start to tell them a story about a young woman who was unjustly fired by a horrible boss, they cross their arms and legs and start raising their eyebrows continuously. It's possible that rather than suddenly feeling negative about you, they are instead responding to the content of your story. Context is always key!

That being said, even if you aren't quite sure what exactly somebody is responding to, reading the signs that they are potentially uncomfortable gives you a huge amount of information about how they might like to be approached. Somebody who is uncomfortable (for any reason) is probably not looking to be pushed or scandalized by a high energy conversation. They are probably looking for some way to feel safe and at ease, which can be done in a variety of ways, depending on how well you know them, and what the situation is.

Using Psychological Skills to Read People

There are a variety of skills we can pull from the world of psychology to help understand and read people. Here are a couple quick tips.

Ask People Thoughtful Questions

This is an incredibly simple skill that almost nobody uses. Studies show that people get more pleasure from talking about themselves than anything else. This can always be used to your advantage. Take charge of a conversation by asking open ended questions, and don't cut people off when they respond. If you give people space to talk, they will almost always surprise you with the depth of information they will give you. In addition, the pleasure centers in their brain will be activated, so they will associate talking to you with positive feelings, even if they can't pinpoint exactly why. Asking people questions will also give you a great opportunity to learn more about people; you can establish a baseline for their behavior, and it also gives you an opportunity to form a genuine connection.

People commonly mistake listening and asking questions as a passive role, but in reality, it's been proven that people who don't ask questions and talk about themselves are perceived two ways: being weak or out of power, or being self-centered and power grabbing. We often want to talk about ourselves in order to show people that we deserve respect, that we are knowledgeable, etc. In reality, we are often doing the exact opposite. Don't forget that up to 97% of our information about other people comes from body language. You don't need to steal the focus of the conversation to prove you are worthy of time and respect. However tempting, don't give in to the desire to correct people, or the desire to "listen" when you are actually just waiting to interrupt with your own agenda. Often in conversation, the question is this: do you want to be right, or do you want to make connections? Every party has the guy who's always right, and you'll find him over in the corner, alone.

Be An Active and Aware Listener

Be aware of your own body language, voice, etc. Listening is not a passive activity, and you are putting out a ton of information while you are listening. Make sure you aren't crossing your arms, rolling your eyes or looking everywhere but at the person's face, checking your watch, cutting them off. These things might seem obvious, but I bet if you observe how you listen to other people, you will probably be surprised at what you find your body doing. The vast majority of people are terrible listeners, and it 100% affects how somebody perceives you, and also the information they give you, and their ability to relax and connect with you.

Observe and Honor Presentational Choices

We all want to be seen positively by the people around us, but above that, we want to be seen honestly as ourselves. For many people, positive identity factors of ethnicity, sexual orientation, geographical location, and other factors are important indicators of who they are and how they move through the world. New research suggests that the most important thing to people is to be seen and affirmed for their identities. Trying to read people's identity (especially without knowing them well) can be a very tricky territory, but there are some factors in presentational choices that can be easily read.

- Insignia, slogans, jewelry, and tattoos. Take into account words or symbols that people display. Take the opportunity to ask them about them.

- Verbal cues. If people mention identity factors that seem like they are important to their identity, make sure you give them space and time to talk about them, and be as interested and affirming as possible. You have everything to gain by making people feel comfortable in their true identity.

Reading People Quickly

For many people, the topic of learning to read people is of most interest for situations where you don't know people and you need to make a good impression quickly. In those circumstances, here's a quick guide to instantly reading and connecting with people. All the other lessons apply, but they can be applied quickly.

- **Enter the room** with the body language and intention you want.
- **Read the room** and respond honestly. What is already happening? Can you tell the

emotion of the room? In general, what's the mood?

- **Read body language** of the person you are interested in talking with. Make eye contact, and smile genuinely and meaningfully.

- **Establish a baseline** of the person you are talking to. If you already know them, use their baseline.

- **Observe your own behavior** and adjust it. Are you putting out the right energy with your voice and body for people to respond to you how you want to be responded to?

- **Ask questions, listen genuinely** and well. Notice changes away from the baseline, and adjust your behavior and questions accordingly.

An Overview

In general, all people are looking for a personal connection, and respond well to feeling safe and valued. The trick to succeeding in almost any interpersonal interaction is to make somebody feel this way without giving up your own power. It is surprisingly easy to make this happen.

Here is a quick recap

- **Know yourself** and what you're looking for in an interaction. Using the questions in the beginning of the article, start to develop a nuanced understanding of who you are in the world, and how that naturally affects how you interact with people. Then, know that each situation is different. Identify what kind of connection you are looking for.

- **Establish a baseline.** Use all available information about somebody to try and find out what their "normal" is. This can include gut impressions, previous interactions, things you know from Wikipedia or a friend, etc. Don't forget to include the immediate environment: temperature, time of day, and what else is happening in the room are very important factors.

- **Read body language** how are they responding to you? How are they responding to other people in the room?

- **Look for word clues.** What people say is important, but it's even more important to see how they choose to say it.

- **Listen. Ask questions. Then listen some more.** Ask people questions about themselves. Ask to follow up questions that show you are listening well. Practice non-judgemental affirmation: respond to show them that you are interested in listening, but don't feel a need to over-empathize or tell them what you think. Your interest is enough.

- **Group clues together.** Since everybody is so different, each situation will be slightly unique. These techniques all work best in tandem: what somebody's body language is saying is easier to understand with a good understanding of their baseline, and somebody's word choice might be completely different when you take into account their body language.

- **Trust yourself!** You will start to develop your own ability to connect with people in your own unique way. You already have all the skills needed, it's just a process of tuning in and refining them. Your gut reactions are actually a highly developed kinesthetic and mental reaction to a lot of information that we aren't used to paying attention to. Above all else, start paying attention to this and trusting it.

So there you have it! A series of tips and ideas to connect

easily, quickly, and genuinely with people, while reading their behavior and language. The practice of reading people is deeply beneficial. It will definitely get you more dates, more friends, and better business connections. You might also find that moving through the world seeking genuine connection doesn't just get you results, but it allows for meaningful relationships, and in that regard, everybody wins!

HOW TO
ANALYZE
PEOPLE
Read People Instantly Using Psychological
Techniques, Social Skills, and Body Language Signals
LUCAS GARRISON

P.S. Thank you for reading this book. If you've enjoyed this book, please don't shy, drop me a line, leave a review or both on Amazon. I love reading reviews and your opinion is extremely important for me.

My Page on Amazon

amazon.com/author/lucasgarrison

www.ingramcontent.com/pod-product-compliance
Lightning Source LLC
Chambersburg PA
CBHW071236240726

48654CB00009B/1070